Paper City

PAPER CITY

a caprice on the subject of disillusionment

Nathalie Stephens

COACH HOUSE BOOKS

first edition

Published with the assistance of the Canada Council for the Arts and the Ontario Arts Council

We acknowledge the Government of Ontario through the Ontario Book Publishers Tax Credit program and through the Ontario Book Initiative.

NATIONAL LIBRARY OF CANADA
CATALOGUING IN PUBLICATION

Stephens, Nathalie, 1970-
Paper city : a caprice on the subject of disillusionment / Nathalie Stephens.

Poems.
ISBN 1-55245-126-7
1. Title.

PS8587.T375P36 2003 C811'.54 C2003-904401-7

A translation is either remarkable
or it is not a translation at all.

These are the body's fictions.

They are artless attempts at formalism.
They are entrenchments, fallacies.

They are mathematically correct and as such of little interest.
What does it matter whether the sum of one and one is two and divisible, when one disappears inside the other?

The body's fictions are *deliberate*

and we are watchful.

Début

n and *b* were in their dictionaries when Art fell. *n* was *néant*. *b* was betwixt. Side by side and at times apart they were glutinous and unlawful. They were referred to in some circles as *necessary evils*. Circumscribed, disregarded, outcast. Scarcely tolerated. The folly ascribed to them served primarily to excise them, to render them *harmless* or *insignificant*.

We have been split at the hoof, n said. Where she went she left marks clippety-clop.

A tear down *b*'s face cleaved it in two.

A century ended one hundred years ago. *Plus ça change.* Demonstrably. A span of time is not equatable with years passed. We have new fonts if little else. The writing on the wall is illegible. *Le cri* is the echo of a drunken frat boy hitting the sidewalk. He lands face first in vomit, oblivious to the dissonance of fallen cities. While his friends identify chunks of carrots and evaluate the quality of bile, ancient walls *s'effritent* immeasurably.

The author is not positing *a better day.*

Merely we are watchful: *nous veillons*.

b produced *Commodify me.* How the Artists swooned! (They had forgotten irony.) Some heard *Come modify me.* They were doubly rapt. They dinned *b's unexpected turn-around!* (Allowing this once for the *minuscule;* for hadn't he too, *enfin,* capitulated?) Indeed he was spinning. With impatience no doubt as *n* saw him off at *la gare.* He was boarding a train and *n* was seeing him off. The city grew impatient for that departure.

Everywhere artists were fucking. They were uncharacteristically immoderate. Art fell further. *n* and *b* grew silent. One waved a white hanky. The other brushed aside a tear. For they courted anachronism. Half-smiles. And the body's curvature as the train pulled out of the station. *n* tucked her soft cock into her skirt. This was no time for jubilation. *n* and *b* were in mourning. Each for the other and individually. The road was long across the ocean and neither had learned to fly outside of sleeping. They were suddenly wide awake. They were slipping from the page. Inconsolably.

From the start they had been unabashed *idéalistes.* They had entrusted their tongues to language and privileged labials over all other sounds. That is, until they were confronted with *la langue's* unmentioned parsimony. They were crest-fallen, each and together, and both refused speaking, inevitably. The consequences were abysmal. *L'abîme,* whispered *n* as she disappeared but not without shaking a fist. They were crossing themselves out of their city: *rayé,e,s.* They had cast themselves against the brashness of white, the flickering screen, the unwritten page, the frothing sea, the blinding snow.

n's last words, as *b* had recorded them, were inaudible.

As they slipped through the broken link of a twisted metal fence, they glanced back at nothing.

The contorted faces of the Artists turned skyward.

At the joining of two streets, a book caught fire. *b* put the match out with his tongue and fluttered his eyes.

The body is heat. Art is desire. Their city had altogether fallen.

Venæ Cavæ

n and *b* were at an etymological disadvantage. They spoke the full weight of words. They were not erudite but careful. That is, they took care in speaking and more particularly in not speaking. Their sentences were cumbersome at times and as a result most refused intercourse with them. Neither *n* nor *b* objected, as they too refused intercourse, although let it be said that they were in the throes of a rather comical miscommunication. A sexual subterfuge. They delighted in the discomfort aroused in their interlocutors, which did not go unnoticed. And although they took pleasure in these peripheral provocations, their vendetta was with Art, more specifically with the Murderers of Art.

Their century had ended without logistical complication. All was well. The gravity of the matter could not have been overstated. *n* and *b* were hollow veins, pumping air into a bloodless heart. Their combined sorrow was cavernous. Their rage incendiary. For a while they knocked about. Into walls, into one another. They were disoriented, estranged. Eventually they grew calm. In reality they were seething. They were but two. One disappeared inside the other. *n* inside of *b*. *b* inside of *n*. They crossed one another out saying *Art lost to numbers.* They were painfully right.

Ménage à Trois

The arrival of ? had been quite unexpected. ? was unnameable and remained such. The elusive quality of ? caused many disturbances in the perfunctorily regimented *Art World* as its partisans insistently referred to it. *b* did suggest the un-name [kwʌt] – an amalgam of the French *quoi* and English *what,* only marginally distorted as he somehow ended up with the Gallic *coït* which *n* found to be unbearably amusing and punctuated her glee by tweaking *b*'s more prominent nipple. ?, who sported every description of genitalia, was unperturbed by the exchange and wished only to sort out sleeping arrangements, explaining not without affect, *Without sleep the body weeps.* Both *n* and *b* synchronized their watches noddingly, returning at once to the matter at hand, which slipped lugubriously through their knotted fingers.

They lived together harmoniously and quite openly for a time, although evidence of linguistic impropriety eventually forced them into hiding. For the blend they had openly assumed, a neither/nor relationship to tongue and its plural antecedents rendered communication with them nearly impossible. *n* and *b* in the company of *?* had admiringly, some whispered, assumed language quite artfully, tearing it from common usage, reducing it in a simmering brew of excess verbiage to its poetic essence, albeit a much debatable point. Inevitably, they were accused of cultishness. Their sexual practices, which were equally slippery, were termed dangerous and, worse, a threat to the *common good*, and they were tracked like rabid dogs. Had they striven for *purity* of expression, that is, had they expressed an exclusive affiliation with one language or another (and its attendant culture), their efforts would have been lauded. They would have been upheld as *the last of a dying race.*

Yes, well. When Art fell, neither *n* nor *b* were anywhere to be seen. Two faint shadows stained the city walls when we caught up with *?*. Our mouths were full of questions, but we hadn't words to speak.

Paper City

Colour is *élogieux*. But the absence of colour offers even greater allure, for desire brings language into being. And colour is an aspect – integral – of language. And integral means not only unperishable – not to be conflated with immortal, which will emerge no doubt in later versions of this same text – but visceral. The *version intégrale* of a work of literature is one that has not been altered, that has not been *tampered with*. They are the author's words as laid down by the author, as assembled and at times dismantled, as manipulated and too as astonished. For let it be said that while language astonishes the writer, the writer too astonishes language. Only the writer who astonishes language – who dares to *tamper* with it – is worthy of the epithet. Language is assuredly the author's tool, but it is also sediment, and when disturbed, may at once muddy and reveal. More importantly, sediment travels, over land, through the body, across the tongue. It is untouchable, and must not be revered.

Language admonishes the body. It fictionalizes desire. It lives inside the body where it takes the place of breath. Eventually it dies there. Encrusted at the corner of the mouth. In the form of drool or a measly crumb. What was sensual and unexpected turns from itself, becomes abject, *indigeste.*

The body is the first poem. Words come later. Eventually there is no need for them at all. The linguistic surge is satisfied

by the existence of the echo.

Interrogatoire

The following inquisitorial dialogue is believed to have been recorded shortly before the disappearance of *n* and *b*. It has been referred to at length and by numerous individuals who *came later* in search of some of the things which prompted their own *evaporation*. Aspects of the dialogue remain unattributed, although the insurgent voices are easily demarkable for the layperson as well as the expert. On occasion, a third voice intervenes. It is the voice of reason. Often it does not interject. It needn't. It is that pervasive.

~ In a paper city write nothing down.

~ These are the walls in which we reside.

~ These are our prisons. Our labyrinths. And they are deadly. (We have no string.)

~ We are insatiable with wanting to find the thing we are looking for. *Our own minotaur.*

~ I challenge you to name it. Name specifically the thing you are looking for. The thing you seek.

~ You ask the impossible. The thing is of little importance. What matters is the *élan,* the reach, that movement toward or away from.

~ You mean to say you are grasping.

~ Grasping nothing. I mean to say that in reaching for a thing we are able to alter the course of literature, of Art. In *settling* for the thing that is already within reach, that is *recognizable, familiar,* we script our own failure – not only do we script it but we agree to that pact – we enact the failure of humanity.

~ So-called.

~ Indeed.

~ Ahem. Humanity?

~ When the artist ceases to be an impostor, when the artist agrees to a *formula*, when the artist sacrifices Art to comfort, to *expectation,* then Art ceases to exist. Beauty is seconded. The paper city burns.

~ Art becomes a fist tightening around the throat.

~ Its sole impulse is pow–

The tape catches. The voices are indistinguishable from one another. All that remains is a single coffee-stained paper transcript of the *interaction*. Authorship has been unattributable to date. No one has been held accountable although many accusations fly unabashedly in the underground, which is where we must begin, if we are to find the slightest trace of either *n* or *b*.

? will be our sometimes guide, grunts and hip thrusts aside.

Digressions Toward Context

The implications of the actions of *n* and *b* are biblical in proportion. Much like that man from Nazareth – who rather than being cut at the throat was purportedly pierced at the joints and other tender places (a sadistic and in some cases admirable aesthetic) and for this unstoppably if stupidly revered etc. etc. – no living being with the exception of *?* who remains speechless to this day could claim with any degree of honesty to have ever been in the company of *n* and *b*. Some claimed to have seen them from afar, through a smoky glass, sometimes across a body of water or climbing onto a bus. A man named Saul lived closest in time to the former politician – that Nazarene – although some thirty years after that unforgotten death. A man he might have *known* had his own prejudices not hindered his own grunts and hip thrusts. His admonishments betray a rather carnal *appétit* for Nazarenes of the male variety, but in good keeping with religious proscription he pushed it all inside with whatever sharp object lay within reach. This all ties quite effortlessly back to *n* and *b* whose spillage elicited the sort of wrath visited upon the Man On The Cross. One is led somewhat inevitably to ponder the question of his sexual habits, which found him snuggling up to one Jonathan and consorting with a whore named Magdalene. Ah love. Here we are then, back at the beginning, touching upon the body, repository and source of every unavowable desire, and subject of (and to) indescribable repression.

When a thing doesn't fit into a box, what is to be done? Neither *n* nor *b* fit into their prescribed boxes. *n*'s words trampled the page, and *b*'s figures came crashing from the canvas onto the lily-white floor. *They blooded art.* This was the accusation flung at them. Which really meant: they brought it to life. Since the day when that Nazarene had gazed at the desert from atop two heavy sticks of wood, human beings have organized against the body, against life. They have coveted the straight line and right angles, and for centuries have busied themselves with the production of boxes into which they have stalwartly insisted on pushing themselves and others too. Human beings are resolute. But who are the producers of these boxes and how have they so succeeded in indenturing the minds of most, who willingly mutilate themselves for the sake of the box?

Art has not been exempt. Left and Right have espoused this hegemony, clamouring *Pick me! Pick me!* So that when *n* and *b* snubbed even their own dictates, the world changed shape, *the Artists* grew faint in the wake of their willing deceit. It is an indisputable truth that in the face of humiliation, humans of every ilk – including *the Artists* – will retaliate.

Sans Issue

Where two rivers converge, one also forks. This had been *n*'s particular experience. She lived at the confluence of two rivers and they both emptied into her mouth. *I open my mouth and drown,* she had been known to say. She was neither of one *rive* nor of the other, and her *appartenance*, while flagrantly resisted, was hotly debated, contested and denied. *Neither* is an unsuitable affiliation and intolerable in a world of boxes, both big and small. This rendered *n*, of course, invisible and led quite naturally to a chance encounter with *b*, who gallantly opened doors for her onto nothing. She was delighted by the subterfuge and so invited him to tea. After a preliminary exchange of violences endured and countries visited, neither of which could be returned to – that is, the country or the past – they forged an enduring *amitié* born in part of contempt for their surrounding worlds, a language fetish and a particular affection for the colour blue. They were sensualist *dépressifs* who experienced society as an affront to their fragile constitutions. Assuredly, they were anachronisms in their high-speed day, at once courting and eschewing the draw of urbanism and its inherent decay. And language was all twisted up in their vision, a great mess of tortuous *voies* which converged against the grey sky pressing down on the city, fastidiously wrought and similarly tormented. For *b* it was simple. He raised his envy-provoking ass to the sky and said *Kiss me. n* was already temperamental by then and took instead to making her body into a palimpsest, carving inscriptions with a fine blade *à même la peau.* It wasn't blood she was after but the certainty of skin closed against itself. Her scarified body was testimony, she said, to an unwilling tongue. She was dreadfully misunderstood and it was some time before *b* was able to extract her from that so-called *maison de repos.*

Walls are erected all the time, for and against. The globe is replete with them and this should be cause for much consideration. Regardless of location, they all conspire to keep one group of people apart from another group of people, and instigate opposition in the guise of security, the focus being on *staying in* rather than *keeping out.* Either way, enemies are made and conflicts ensue. Someone drops a bomb.

Some time before her *appréhension, n* wandered into a book-shop. It was one she frequented quite regularly. She was aghast. There, before her, was *l'intégralité* of her personal collection, and somehow, without her knowledge, it had migrated. She could, of course, lay claim to none of it. She hurried home at once, stopping only to call *b* along the way, but he had been sitting on her doorstep all afternoon, documenting the transition of the sky from white to grey. It was to be his masterpiece of visual fiction, a dissident tableau that would offend the proponents of colour. The *Art World* was not ready for *nuance.* They sat all evening with one lit candle in an empty room. The walls were bare. *n*'s script had been torn from her mouth. *b* draped a thin arm over her shoulders and with the other gestured toward the walls acknowledging *Le néant. n* waited for the echo. It was right there before her and she hadn't seen it. A tear slid into her mouth. They fell asleep casting shadows.

O E dans l'O(rifice) or Œ

To the underground then. Beneath every city is an intricate network of tunnels, some of which are regularly put to use while others are forgotten for decades sometimes centuries at a time, until a person in search of adventure happens upon an unusual stench and proceeds to investigate. Some of Europe's abandoned subway stations are veritable time capsules, museums of undisturbed graffiti and the odd forgotten *publicité.* The twenties' hollow roar permeates walled-off parts of Paris's *Métropolitain* and the *Résistance* follows to this day its uninterrupted course. Even North America has its own buried *réseaux* of sewers and other secret passages. All it takes on a dark night is a pry bar, a strong set of muscles and narrow hips to wander where Alice never did. Grime does have its appeal and in a world that venerates perfection, a revolt is easily instigated with a pail of mud and a hand-built catapult.

Were *?* able to speak, words would emerge with a slur. Not a drunken slur but a slanderous one, a slur in the sense of an offence, an *injure*, a litany of disdain, for *?*'s demeanour alone exuded untempered contempt. Therein lay *?*'s ineffable likeability.

We did not begin at the mouth of the city's underneath, nor at any of its more dubious orifices. Camus's rats had beat us to it and there was no sense in pursuing a literal line of thought. We would not have merited even the search. While sipping coffee early in the afternoon at the end of a prolonged night of pleasurable digressions in the company of *?*, we admiringly if inadvertently stuttered over a diphthong. It had kabbalistic appeal. Its sinuosity recalled the coil of muscle snaking around *n*'s forearm and the curl in *b*'s spine. Its mystery conveyed obeisance to no known or knowable rule of law. The diphthong is nearly an elision, a seductive glide from one letter sound to another, neither of which retains its autonomy or purity of sound, neither of which is discernible as such. Linguistically speaking, the diphthong is in abeyance. It is a ligature, an intimate gesture of language. It taunts (*taints*) the tongue with its own form of echo and its ultimate disappearance. *Il brouille les pistes.* It embroils the tongue in a sort of polysemic disloyalty. The body that takes heed need only follow.

Our snouts to the ground we came first upon the scent of an elision, and wondrously pursued it deep into the lidded eye's fold. We swam bodily. We were in tears.

( )

M documents everything. *M* is Mark. She has a camera on each arm and one hanging from her neck. Her main disadvantage is lack of film, although when we first caught up with her at the local branch of the public library, she was busily developing her rolls. Regardless, she does not know *n* or *b*. She was born many many years later, but her temporal displacement matters little. She is the only public authority on the subject, as she has received much private funding for her filmic documentary, *Sodomy Ro(gu)e.* Says she (she is clearly a follower of both reticent artists), what imports most is that which withdraws from the image, and as such, film seems to her an unnecessary expense. She lives under the *bombé* bridge beneath a turtle shell. It reminds her of home.

(The evidence is perhaps tangential. Some might go so far as to say *tendencieux*. The tone is accusatory. Allow please for this interjection: if in order to touch upon a thing it is necessary to *stretch* far enough to reach it, has the body been engaged in contortions, or is it merely fitting itself into a new shape? And perhaps more pointedly, does the attempt – *la tentative* – to assume a new shape, one that moves both outside and in, not constitute its own completion? The *élan* in which both movement and desire are achieved through and outside of)

the body.

’

In French, *apostrophe* is a verb. The action is direct and involves the injury of one’s interlocutor with words. What it gives it takes away. As does the noun form which engages the omission of a letter or sound, surfacing often in contractions of all muscles (not excluding the sphincter) and the ensuing shortening of sentences. This to accommodate the need for one world superpower to trademark its own *New Sentence Order* (in patents we trust!) and thus enact *highspeed* as a new currency. Still, words must be pronounced and orders resisted. Such an interaction, depicted graphically, might look something like this:

~ p*nch p*nch

~ p*nch p*nch

~ * *

~ * *

in which neither participant *wins* as such, although the extraction from the quotidian of one participant often inspires a great deal of suspicion and absolute reticence to provide details as to their whereabouts for fear of following in their *wake*. Such is the autocracy of language as decried by *n* and *b* in a seminal treatise on the calamity of speech, published by Noose Editions in a hand-bound limited edition of three (one each plus a floater). It is miraculously available for public viewing during off hours in Room C. Regrettably, however, the clerk in charge of that particular collection is on permanent leave. He too spoke out of turn. His sentence was mild: regular semi-colonic irrigation. This helps neither you the Reader, nor we the Maudlin, nor they the Author nor he that Nazarene who remains to this day *much punctuated* and is of little relevance to either *n* or *b* and as such ourselves, we the Above.

Despite this inconvenience, we do have in our possession the knowledge of both the title and inscription on the first and subsequent pages of the treatise. They are as follows:

Title: Eighteen Letters to the Reader

Turn Around.
Bend Over.

Together we have been many places and seen many beautiful things sometimes even people.

Some Faint Impressions (most of which have since been washed away)

Before *n*'s arrival, the city had been terse. This was not just her own observation but the observation of others as well. With this difference: *the others liked it that way.* It was, after all, or so they maintained, their city. Terse was not wordless but close enough and *n* was not, as has been gleaned from her *mémoire* (most of which has been erased), a proponent of restraint. Nor was she, however, fond of wastefulness, and she was struck in the face by the concurrent existence in the city that was for her to become a paper city of both excessive verbosity (*waste*) – which took the form of idle talk, the publication *en masse* of many plot-driven novels and most misguidedly of all *selfhelpbooks* (the purpose of all of which was to *flatulate*) – and a glaring absence of emotion (*restraint*), which manifested itself in brashly coloured walls, bright artificial foods, floors lit green or yellow or orange from underneath and excessive gesticulation all of which to mask the lack of substance in the lives that were being lived. That is until the first and subsequent floods, none of which can be attributed to either *n* or *b* despite historical (im)posturing. At which time the city went soggy and even the most deluged of its citizens were unable to summon its previous flair. Shortly thereafter *n* is rumoured to have said (not without reference to a previous and similarly testy work) *Après moi la parole.* She was not averse to eating her words and would do it again if only to demonstrate the inextricability of vocables from the body to which they return. Dust to dust and all that, but she was adamant there was nothing *Adamic* about her refusal at times to speak. Merely, she was biding her time, and as she exemplified on numerous discomfiting occasions, there are many things to do with one's mouth besides speaking.

Hearsay (Heresy)

Is it possible to come from nowhere? *La Provenance,* said *n* and fell away from sleep. She saw herself especially but others as well as unravelling. Like a knitted sweater perhaps or an intricacy of fraying wires. Except those parts of her that unravelled or came away disappeared altogether. As though in *coming away* she was left with nothing to show for it. The implications of this particular predicament were disconcerting. It meant she had only the things before her which meant that in effect she had nothing was nothing and would amount to nothing. What some might term freedom.

Is it possible to live only in the present? Glaringly, no. The sum of other moments being the most obvious refutation. But further still, the accumulation in time of places overlapping and a zeal for travel. With *b* on his train and that great engine in his hip *n* remained with a mouth full of smoke and the grumble of locomotion. The vibrations of metal and earth clanged inside her, disturbing the bones of her body from their usual configuration, allowing momentarily for the belief that by necessity and for the sake of continuity, Art must have no loyalty. Translated of course into actions that precede both body and tongue, and much like the train carrying *b* far from *la gare* in which moments before he stood murmuring parting words into *n*'s ringing ears, remain incessantly on the verge of thinning from view into a thick but untouchable cloud of black smoke. Leading some to conclude: *Art is a thing of the past.* Words scrawled in thick red ink on the underside of the train. And being that the past does not exist and as such exists infinitely, it too will be forgotten before long.

Her Paper City would be mute. It could not be made to speak. This much *n* surmised from the chatter in her feet. *Beauty!* she scoffed, pulling an iron scaffolding away from a tall skinny house. She railed against imagism while kicking a tin can along the road. Her belief was infinite. And because of this it was hollow. Hollow perhaps but not empty. It held only one certainty: that a thing in the process of becoming was already fast disappearing. And rather than try so desperately to hold it all in place with the aid of contracts or idle threats or loose string, would it not benefit everyone involved to *just let go.*

She offered the following cases in point:

1 *S* was solicitude. He had been caught buggering his neighbour's husband while murmuring sweet nothings into his ear. The whole neighbourhood was in on the act so to speak, as his cries rose above the din of TV dinners and other forms of conjugal inanity. Still, he vowed chastity to his wife, who was no longer dupe and said in reply to his errancy, *S, I have a buggerer of my own.* Leaving the cold wind blowing onto his bare muscled ass as she emptied the house into the car and drove off in search of a more brightly coloured town.

2 Three were Tapioca and three were Buxom and the generally accepted practice was for each Tapioca to encircle their designated Buxom while among themselves Buxom could circulate quite freely even laughingly as long as they maintained certain understood limits urges notwithstanding. In the company of Tapioca and Buxom, Feelers were considered anathema as their practice was tentacular owing only to their irrepressible need to know. One such Feeler was inadvertently invited to a dinner party of three pairs of Tapioca-Buxom, all of whom became squeamish and glared fearfully in the Feeler's direction, in whose defence it must be said had eyes neither for Tapioca nor their Buxom as they lacked each and together, well, fuckability. Nonetheless,

egocentrism in tow, the six all banded together, and in keeping with historical practice had the one Feeler apprehended and sequestered into a small squared-off concrete cubicle where various aversion therapies were duly administered and from which the Feeler emerged smilingly if limbless.

3 Bite me.

n's *exposé* was irrefutable.

Everything she saw bled through.

The city was unprepared for such insolent disloyalty.

Before Langue

The following words were *n*'s before they were anyone else's. They were addressed, although to whom remains unknown, speculation notwithstanding. She was a fetishist of the fold and understandably kept such things to herself:

> *Je veux l'intraduisible.*

And underneath:

> *I want what no language holds.*

n's distress was enviable. She knew what was missing. Her accounts had been frozen. Her apartment seized. And all of her effects – all but her books which had already found their way to the creaking shelves of an old bookshop – taken away. When left with nothing but the body one pays attention. And that *n* did. She traced her agony back to a letraset given to her as a child. This did nothing to offset the anguish of betrayal. But at least she knew what she was up against. *b* was long gone by then, leaning from his apartment balcony into his own river watching this time for his city to turn from grey to white. He saw everything double. To which has been attributed his great foresight in predicting and subsequently enacting his own and *n*'s disappearance.

They wrote feverishly to one another and at times not at all going great stretches without contact each confronting their respective cities alone. *b* said *Sola*. A fervent echo to the hammer blow in *n*'s heart. *A language must be lived.* This perhaps the greatest cruelty of all. For the body needed salvaging somehow. The body in its city. Burning. Together they were burning. All eyes turned away.

Frondes

For *b* the matter changed hands quite regularly. While the city had come into *n*, *b* had come into the city. This on the one hand had made it possible for *b* to leave and on the other had made *n*'s remaining inevitable. It didn't really matter where *n* went her city would follow her there. For it was everywhere. What then of *n*'s untranslatability? We began at the uppermost hole of a pegboard stashed between two brick buildings, one of which leaned into the other casting a damp shadow over everything we attempted to see. We nonetheless prodded with our narrowest fingers some of us with our tongues and out came a comma. *Aha!* we exclaimed. And the buildings echoed our excitement by shouting *Aha!* right back. We had found something.

The issue remained: what to do with it. At which point we stumbled upon *e* or rather *e* upon us as we were all leaning into the alley obstructing the sidewalk with our back ends. *e* was elusive. Not surprising really. And unlike *?* who was all aflame *e* disappeared into the body that housed the mind leaving no indication as to the whereabouts or wherefroms of this unwrought letter. *Once I was le féminin,* said *e* not wistfully but with a tinge of remorse underscoring a vanishing emotion with the flick of what may very well have been a tail.

So began a long story of sorrow that made itself indistinguishable from a comfortable warm liquid that to *e* was akin to an aura, imperceptible perhaps but wetting us nonetheless. *e* made no claims to having ever known *n* and scorned our search, saying we had only to look to our own names for the shapes of even the most confounding of letters.

Delectably *e* recounted the tale of the comma which to *n* had been a *glissement* from word to word and sometimes letter to letter and even from body to body making one indistinguishable from the other confusing limbs with other features somewhat like what Picasso did to his figures although with less butchery but no less madness wanting for the body the same freedom that language might have held. *e* paused here allowing us to absorb the fatalism of the lingering words. Wishing the conditional out of the sentence, the sentence being full of conditions and all conditions having been met, we wept.

,

In a yet unpublished paper on the Comma, what *n* preferred to call a *take*, writing *la virgule* virulently, what no Critic would dare call *une thèse virulente*, all Critics being bound to those same Artists (interchangeably), that remained *hors circuit*, each word placed in apposition to the other not undeserving of the ire of those to whom it was directed, namely those proponents of *le bon usage* (coughcough), fragmented,

She put forward these *marmonnements* – malice on the tongues of those who scorn speech that originates in the body.

1 Comma not separator nor
2 pause for nor
3 breath at times
4 *une interruption* oh! (as in) and simultaneously
5 that very desirable *glissement*

stopping at five as before the assembly she moved her body across the floor shedding clothes exposing where berries once grew the seductions of a *ventouse* and *b* right behind her his whole glistening body decorated with a medley of pink *méduses*. Those gathered were stung by the audacity of their presenters (claiming indisputable ownership) and in leaving were heard uttering the words *taken in*. And yes they had. And yes they had been. And were. There was no going back to their bodies now. Not like before.

For a brief moment a faint light sparked the night sky and on billboards everywhere the following words:

'le, corps, remémoré, est, d'une, fragilité,'

n's books were skin. Paper and bone. *b*'s pictures were blood with all the colour gone.

Sands

We soon wrote off *?*'s gyrations as superfluous. Immense fun but carrying us no further along in our desire to *know*. We had followed the movement of *?*'s hips into the most colourful clubs in the remotest of places and were met each time with greater noise thinking nonetheless this is where *n* sat. This is where *b* danced. This is the place where the moon shone the brightest over their untempered gesticulations. Where *?* went we went for we were looking for something we had yet to find.

In a bistro at the edge of the water we sat one morning over bowls of steaming black coffee. The previous night's transgressions cut lines into the face of *?* who sat heavily at the table hiccuping and trembling sometimes laughingly sometimes with scorn. Night cleared eventually from *?*'s face emerging from the one hollow hip and bursting biliously out of that pasty mouth. *?* had brought us to the desert. From that sometimes sullen and often undecided body had emerged another landscape into which we dove vicariously each of us seeking the thing we thought we would find.

We turned over a large stone revealing a smudge of charred words:

'La nuit le désert fléchit.'

The earth turned red by the scourge of History, bodies tumbling over one another wanting another script. For where it began it ended just as abruptly tongue-tied and yearning for other words   home.

We had found the tomb of time, a cry wrenched from the viscera, body buckled, mouth opening onto a wild and murderous dream. The script was indecent.

We took off our shoes and walked barefoot the rest of the way.

Wince

Revolt. There is no such truth. One word spears the tongue. Soon another will follow. Dictatorships are interchangeable. History is repetition. And the gloss of interpretation confers an equal number of losses. Power. Who will write it down? The Cabaret not the University arouses the intellect. And both lull the mind one with spirits the other with theory. *I never loved you anyway.* That is the nature of betrayal. That of the body by language. That of Art by the people. That of nature by greed. That of desire by scorn. And so on. Line. Someone draws a line. *We all fall d(r)own.*

Lessons (Lessens)

A poet who is said to be great, most often in hindsight, is said to have lived before his time. *What time is it?*

The intent is to exonerate the poet's contemporaries for being so bludgeoningly stupid or cruel or vindictive or spiteful or genocidal or complacent or willing or

The intent is to exonerate oneself for being so clueless or unobservant or simpering or undecided or opportunistic or complicit or

The emotion is sentimental as though only from a great distance might one risk feeling.

The movement, although in appearances one of solidarity, is one of disavowal or separation or distinction as though by underscoring difference through approval one gives only the appearance of approval.

If then. But you weren't there. And now. *What about now?*

Who will speak for you?

Will you speak for yourself?

And the body. Who will speak for the body?

Scène

In the Seine many bodies have drowned. In and outside of *Letters*. We too have our rivers for the damned. When peering into water, whose face is reflected back at you? History admonishes all who dare to look. And the rest of you? Twice damned for looking away.

Incendiary words. But language is *of the body*. What breathes burns. What survives burning drowns. And we are reckless.

Erre (Ère)

Where we went neither *n* nor *b* had been. No measure of time could account for their existence. No story told retold untold or even mistold could hold either of them to their *parcours*. Nor the existence of *?* although entertaining provided substantial proof of their having been held in this or that city, of their having pushed against these walls or those. They were gone. *Disparu,e,s*. Or were we misleading ourselves (once again)? Were we the ones who had *gone missing? n* and *b* had *left us behind*. We pulled beds away from walls. We furrowed into the riverbed. We scratched peeling paint away from new metal to expose a welcome sheen underneath. We raked ashes across exhausted flower beds and planted seeds in the caked-dry soil. Where there was colour we washed it away. Where a surface was bare we covered it up. We went to quiet cafés they had purportedly frequented. We sat in chairs said to have been warmed by their bottoms. We danced furiously to rhythms they once lauded. We wore clothing to resemble them. We invented their ghosts to appease the burn in our abdomens the ache in our searching brains. What we touched upon was ours alone. *n* and *b* were letters carved into water. They belonged to no one. Not to those who had cast them out nor to those who would search for them again and again. The city would mourn them as only a city that had driven them out – *disappeared them* – could.

Bend

From the bridge *n* watched the city sprawl.

b was behind her and between them a cushion of air.

Immeasurably

Anne-Marie Alonzo – Marguerite Andersen – derek beaulieu – Stan Bevington – Sylvie Bompis – Antanas Linas Bugailiškis (a.k.a. Tony Boog) – Jason Brown – Ken Clark – Joel Felix – Faye Guenther – Suzanne Hancock – Claire Heslop – Mela Luna – Curt Lush – Kit Malo (genuflecting l'entre-genre) – Phil Masters – Jason McBride – rob mclennan – Jay MillAr – Brane Mozetič – Peter and Michael O'Leary – Benny Nemerofsky Ramsay – Rick/Simon – Amanda Stephens – Francine and Paul Stephens – John Stout – John Tipton – R. M. Vaughan – Darren Wershler-Henry – Alana Wilcox – Ryan Woodward – Rachel Zolf –

Dale

et les animaux

with oblique reference to :
hivernale (GREF, 1995)
L'embrasure (TROIS, 2002)
Le dortoir de l'indiscrétion (inédit)
La blessure (inédit)

To *b* of course

About the Author

Nathalie Stephens writes in English and French, and sometimes neither. She is the author, notably, of *Je Nathanaël* (l'Hexagone, 2003), *All Boy* (housepress, 2001), *Somewhere Running* (Arsenal Pulp, 2000), *Colette m'entends-tu?* (TROIS, 1997) and *This Imagined Permanence* (Gutter, 1996). *UNDERGROUND* (TROIS, 1999) was shortlisted in 2000 for the Grand Prix du Salon du livre de Toronto. In 2002, Nathalie was awarded the distinction of a Chalmers Arts Fellowship. Excerpts from her work have been translated into English and Slovene. She has translated R. M. Vaughan into French and Catherine Mavrikakis into English. On occasion, Nathalie translates herself. Her city, too, is on fire.

Typeset in Granjon
Printed and bound at the Coach House
on bpNichol Lane, 2003

Edited by Jay Millar
Copy edited by Alana Wilcox

Cover image: *Kisses Like Letterforms*, mixed media on paper, 2003, by Benny Nemerofsky Ramsay

Coach House Books
401 Huron Street (rear) on bpNichol Lane
Toronto Ontario
M5S 2G5

416 979 2217
1 800 367 6360

mail@chbooks.com
www.chbooks.com